SPANISH
for
Xenophobes®

Drew Launay

⓪
Oval Books

Published by Oval Books
335 Kennington Road
London SE11 4QE
United Kingdom

Telephone: +44 (0)20 7582 7123
Fax: +44 (0)20 7582 1022
E-mail: info@ovalbooks.com
Web site: www.ovalbooks.com

Published 2003
Reprinted 2005, 2006

Language consultant – Chloe Varella
Illustrator – Charles Hemming
Editor – Catriona Tulloch Scott
Series Editor – Anne Tauté
Cover designers – Jim Wire; Vicki Towers
Printer – Gopsons Papers Ltd.
Producer – Oval Projects Ltd.

In certain instances, the Spanish in this book
has been simplified for easier communication.

The Xenophobe's® Guide to The Spanish
makes the perfect companion to this
Xenophobe's® Lingo Learner.

Xenophobe's® is a Registered Trademark.

ISBN-13: 978-1-903096-19-2
ISBN-10: 1-903096-19-7

Contents

Introduction

When abroad you have to expect foreigners. Most of these foreigners will not speak English. Worse, to them, you are the foreigner.

This phrase book is to help you overcome this setback and cope with the unexpected difficulties that may arise should you need to communicate with the natives.

Phrases are given in English. Then Spanish in *italics*. Then the pronunciation for the English tongue is set out in **bold** type.

Speedy Spanish can make all the difference. The faster you say the bits in bold, the bolder you will become, and thus convince the natives that what they are hearing is in fact their own language.

Pronunciation

Spanish is phonetic, all vowels are pronounced.

i   is pronounced '**ee**'
e   is pronounced '**eh**'.

So *impermeable* (waterproof) is pronounced **eem pair meh ah bleh** and *condones* (condoms) is pronounced **con doe nehs**. Therefore the phrase:

Madre mia, ninguno de estos condones son impermeables

Oh dear, none of these condoms are waterproof

is pronounced:

Ma dreh / mee ah / neen goo no / deh / ess toss / con doe nehs / son / eem pair meh ah blehs.

j   is pronounced like an '**h**' when you have a sore throat, e.g: Juan as in Don Juan – **Don / Who won**.

1

ll (double 'l') is pronounced **ya, yeh, yee, yo** or **you** depending on the letter that follows it, e.g:

llegadas – arrivals – **yeah gard ass**
lluvia – rain –**you vee ah**.

h is not pronounced at all, e.g:

ant – *hormiga* – **or mee ga**.

b and '*v*' can be a great source of bewilderment, even to the Spanish themselves. They sound exactly the same. The translation of Baron (an aristocrat) is *Barón*. The translation for man or male is *Varón*. So the phrase:

The baron's wife has given birth to a male child.
La esposa del Barón dio a luz a un Varón.

can sound like:

La esposa del Varón dio a luz a un Barón.
The man's wife has given birth to a Baron.

n with a wavelet on top (ñ) is pronounced **knee eh** with a slight leaning towards whatever vowel follows it – **knee ah, knee oh** – e.g:

ñangotarse – to be in a squatting position – **knee anne go tar seh**.

au is pronounced '**ow**', as if you had just pricked your finger, e.g:

autobombar – to blow one's own trumpet – **ow toe bomb bar**.

g is hard unless it is in front of an '*e*' or an '*i*' when it has to sound like a cat hissing with its mouth full of mouse e.g:

2

Generally, my pet gorilla loves sunflowers.
Generalmente a mi gorila favorito le gusta los gira-soles.
Hen err al mente / ah / mee / gor ee lah / favor eat toe / leh / goose sta / los / hear ah sol ehs.

ue together after the letter '*g*' are pronounced '**eh**'. So the beer named San Miguel, is not pronounced **San Mig oo well**, but **San Mee gell**.

ui together after the letter '*q*' are pronounced '**ee**', e.g:

mosquito – the flying terror – **moss kee toe**.

z is pronounced '**th**', as though you were spitting, e.g:

zigzaguear – to walk unsteadily – **thig thag eh are**.

Spoken Spanish varies everywhere. In Galicia the accents are clear, in Andalucia confused and, within Andalucia, that spoken in Granada is different to that spoken in Seville. For example, the Spanish for fish is *pescado* (**pess ka doe**). In parts of Andalucia they say *pecao* (**peck cow**). It's best to carry on regardless.

3

The Alphabet

Though the Spanish are not generally interested in other people's personal details, you may need to spell your name for a form, or to give it over the telephone. For this you should know the sounds of individual letters:

A	**ah**	H	**atch ee**	N	**en eh**	U	**ooh**
B	**beh**	I	**ee**	O	**oh**	V	**ooveh**
C	**seh**	J	**hotter**	P	**peh**	W	does not exist
D	**deh**	K	**kah**	Q	**coo**	in the Spanish
E	**eh**	L	**ell**	R	**air eh**	alphabet
F	**eh feh**	LL	**eh yeh**	S	**essay**	Y	**ee gree egg ah**
G	**heh**	M	**em meh**	T	**teh**	Z	**thet ah**

A Bit of Important Grammar

In English the question "Are you alone?" can be asked of a boy or a girl. In Spanish the question has two versions.

Está solo? **Ess tah / so low?** for a male.
Está sola? **Ess tah / so lah?** for a female.

Should you be male and get them wrong by asking *Está sola?* of a young man, you could be in deep trouble.

Possible Pitfalls

Peine	**Pay neh**	means comb
Pene	**Peh neh**	means penis
Cajones	**Ca ho nez**	means drawers
Cojines	**Co he nez**	means cushions
Cojones	**Co ho nez**	means testicles

4

Essential Words to Remember

Very nearly everything can be mimed. You can nod your head for 'yes'. Shake your head for 'no'. You can hold up fingers for numbers, and point rudely at anything you wish to indicate. You cannot, however, mime colours, the past, the present or the future.

If you lost a red suitcase at a railway station yesterday, you can convey lost by looking desperate, suitcase by drawing a square in the air and miming a hand gripping it, you can convey a railway station by making a noise like a locomotive, but red and yesterday are tricky. The following should therefore be kept handy.

Black	*Negro*	**Neh grow**
White	*Blanco*	**Blank oh**
Red	*Rojo*	**Roe ho**
Yellow	*Amarillo*	**Ama ree yo**
Green	*Verde*	**Vair deh**
Blue	*Azul*	**Ah thool**
Brown	*Marrón*	**Ma ron**
Yesterday	*Ayer*	**Ay air**
Today	*Hoy*	**Oy**
Tomorrow	*Mañana*	**Man knee ah nah**

This last is probably the most utilised word in the Spanish language for it not only means tomorrow, but some time tomorrow. The day after tomorrow. The day after that. Next week. Next month. Maybe next month. Next year. Possibly next year. Best think in terms of the next few decades.

You may also need the phrase:

That is not mine.
Eso no es mío.
Esso / no / ess / me oh.

Less Essential But Jolly Useful Words and Phrases

Yes	*Sí*	**Sea**
No	*No*	**No**
Please	*Por favor*	**Paw / fav awe**
Thank you	*Gracias*	**Grassy ass**
Many thanks	*Muchas gracias*	**Mooch ass / grassy ass**
Hello	*Hola*	**Oh lah**
Goodbye	*Adiós*	**Ah dee oss**
Good Morning	*Buenos días*	**Boo eh nose / dee ass**
Good Afternoon	*Buenas tardes*	**Boo en ass / tar dez**
Good Night	*Buenas noches*	**Boo en ass / no chess**

Sod off.
Vete a tomar por culo.
Vet teh / ah / toe mar / paw / cool oh.

Excuse me	*Perdóneme*	**Pear don eh meh**
Forgive me	*Discúlpeme*	**Dis cool peh meh**
Sorry	*Lo siento*	**Low / see en toe**

Frightfully sorry.
Lo siento, lo siento.
Low / see en toe, / low / see en toe.

Toilets (always an embarrassing one to mime):
Servicios **Sair vee sea oss** or, *Aseos* **Ass eh oss**.

Small Talk

Isn't it a beautiful day?
Qué día precioso?
Keh / dee ah / press sea oh so?

Or, to cover all contingencies from 'It's a bit warm today', to 'I can't stand this heatwave':

What heat!
Qué calor!
Keh / cal law!

Numerals

One	*Uno*	**Ooh no**
Two	*Dos*	**Doss**
Three	*Tres*	**Trehs**
Four	*Cuatro*	**Coo ah trow**
Five	*Cinco*	**Sink oh**
Six	*Seis*	**Say ease**
Seven	*Siete*	**Sea eh teh**
Eight	*Ocho*	**Otch oh**
Nine	*Nueve*	**Noo eh veh**
Ten	*Diez*	**Dee eth**

Eleven	*Once*	**On seh**
Twelve	*Doce*	**Doss eh**
Thirteen	*Trece*	**Trehs eh**
Fourteen	*Catorce*	**Cat or seh**
Fifteen	*Quince*	**Keen seh**
Sixteen	*Dieciseis*	**Dee essy say ease**
Seventeen	*Diecisiete*	**Dee essy see eh teh**
Eighteen	*Dieciocho*	**Dee essy otch oh**
Nineteen	*Diecinueve*	**Dee essy noo eh veh**
Twenty	*Veinte*	**Vain teh**
Twenty one	*Veintiuno*	**Vain tea ooh no … etc.**

Thirty	*Treinta*	**Train ta**
Forty	*Cuarenta*	**Coo ah renta**
Fifty	*Cincuenta*	**Sink went ah**
Sixty	*Sesenta*	**Seh senta**

Seventy	*Setenta*	**Seh tenta**
Eighty	*Ochenta*	**Otch enta**
Ninety	*Noventa*	**No venta**

One hundred	*Cien*	**Sea en**
Two hundred	*Doscientos*	**Dos see en toss**
Three hundred	*Trescientos*	**Trehs see en toss** …etc.

| One thousand | *Mil* | **Mill** |
| Two thousand | *Dos mil* | **Doss / mill** …etc. |

| One hundred thousand | *Cien mil* | **Sea en / mill** |
| One million | *Un millón* | **Oon / mill yon** |

Time *La Hora* La / Oar rah

Morning	*Mañana*	**Man knee ah nah**
Night	*Noche*	**Notch eh**
Midday	*Mediodía*	**Med ee ah dee ah**
Midnight	*Medianoche*	**Med ee ah notch eh**

Nine o'clock. *Las nueve.* **Lass / noo eh veh.**

Quarter past nine. *Las nueve y cuarto.*
Lass / noo eh veh / ee / coo are toe.

Twenty past nine. *Las nueve y veinte.*
Lass / noo eh veh / ee / vain teh.

Half past nine. *Las nueve y media.*
Lass / noo eh veh / ee / med dee ya.

Quarter to ten. *Las diez menos cuarto.*
Lass / dee eth / men oss / coo are toe.

Ten a.m. *Las diez de la mañana.*
Lass / dee eth / de / la / man knee ah nah.

Ten p.m. *Las diez de la noche.*
Lass / dee eth / de / la / notch eh.

Days of the Week, etc.

A day	*Un día*	**Oon / dee ah**
Two days	*Dos días*	**Doss / dee ass**
A week	*Una semana*	**Oon ah / sem ah nah**
A fortnight	*Quince días*	**Keen seh / dee ass**
Three weeks	*Tres semanas*	**Trehs / sem ah nass**
Monday	*Lunes*	**Loo nez**
Tuesday	*Martes*	**Mar tez**
Wednesday	*Miércoles*	**Mee air co les**
Thursday	*Jueves*	**Hoo eh vez**
Friday	*Viernes*	**Vee air nez**
Saturday	*Sábado*	**Sah bah doe**
Sunday	*Domingo*	**Domingo**
A month	*Un mes*	**Oon / mess**
Two months	*Dos meses*	**Doss / messes**
A year	*Un año*	**Oon / anne knee oh**
Two years	*Dos años*	**Doss / anne knee oss**
January	*Enero*	**Eh neh roe**
February	*Febrero*	**Feh breh roe**
March	*Marzo*	**Mars oh**
April	*Abril*	**Ah brill**
May	*Mayo*	**My oh**
June	*Junio*	**Who knee oh**
July	*Julio*	**Who lee oh**
August	*Agosto*	**Ah goss toe**
September	*Septiembre*	**Sep tee em breh**
October	*Octubre*	**Ock too breh**
November	*Noviembre*	**No vee em breh**
December	*Diciembre*	**Dee see em breh**
Spring	*Primavera*	**Pree ma vair ah**
Summer	*Verano*	**Veh ra no**
Autumn	*Otoño*	**Oh ton knee oh**
Winter	*Invierno*	**Een vee air no**

The Family *La Familia* La / Fa mee lee yah

Whether you like it or not, sooner or later you will be introduced to someone's vast family. You should therefore know the following:

Mother	*Madre*	**Mad reh**
Father	*Padre*	**Pa dreh**
Daughter	*Hija*	**Ee ha**
Son	*Hijo*	**Ee ho**
Grandmother	*Abuela*	**Ah boo ell ah**
Grandfather	*Abuelo*	**Ah boo ell oh**
Granddaughter	*Nieta*	**Knee et ah**
Grandson	*Nieto*	**Knee et oh**
Sister	*Hermana*	**Air man ah**
Brother	*Hermano*	**Air man oh**
Wife	*Esposa*	**Ess pose ah**
Husband	*Marido*	**Ma ree doe**
Mother-in-law	*Suegra*	**Sue egg rah**
Father-in-law	*Suegro*	**Sue egg roe**
Sister-in-law	*Cuñada*	**Coo knee ah dah**
Brother-in-law	*Cuñado*	**Coo knee ah doe**
Aunt	*Tía*	**Tea ah**
Uncle	*Tío*	**Tea oh**
Niece	*Sobrina*	**Sob reen ah**
Nephew	*Sobrino*	**Sob reen oh**
First cousin (female)	*Prima*	**Preem ah**
First cousin (male)	*Primo*	**Preem oh**

How do you do. (Roman: Pleased to meet you.)
Encantado de conocerle (if you are male).
Encantada de conocerle (if you are female).
En can tard oh / deh / con oh sair leh.
En can tard ah / deh / con oh sair leh.

10

Why does your mother look at me that way?
Porqué me mira así tu madre?
Pork eh / meh / mee rah / ass see / too / mad reh?

With the confidence you have now acquired by using English to speak Spanish you should be able to tackle the following:

At eleven o'clock on a lovely Spring morning in April my mother-in-law's aunt cooked a paella for sixteen people, but my grandfather ate it all and was very sick on the following Wednesday.

A las once de la mañana un precioso dia primaveral de Abril, la tía de mi suegra cocinó una paella para dieciseis personas pero mi abuelo se la comió toda y estuvo muy enfermo el miércoles siguiente.

Work out the pronunciation for yourself.

11

Emergencies   *Urgencias*   Oor hen sea ass

Help! *Socorro!* **Sock orrow!**

Call for a doctor.
Llama a un médico.
Ya ma / ah / oon / meh dick oh.

Call for an ambulance.
Llama a una ambulancia.
Ya ma / ah / oon ah / am boo lancia.

Call for the police.
Llama a la guardia.
Ya ma / ah / la / goo are dee ah.

Call for a funeral director.
Llama al director de pompas fúnebres.
Ya ma / al / dee wreck tor / de / pomp ass / foo neh brez.

I am allergic to peanuts – prawns – nitro glycerine.
Soy alérgico a los cacahuetes – las gambas – la nitro glicerina.
**Soy / al air hee co / ah / loss / cack ah wet tess – lass
gum bass – la / knee tro / glee serene ah**.

I may be about to be sick – collapse – give birth.
A lo mejor voy a vomitar – a colapsar – a dar a luz.
**Ah / low / meh haw / voy / ah / vom mee tar – ah /
collapse ah – ah / dar / ah / looth**.

Please contact my relatives. The address is in my pocket.
*Por favor poneros en contacto con mi familia. La dirección
está en mi bolsillo.*
**Paw / fav awe / pon eh ross / en / con tact oh / con / mee /
fa mee lee yah. / La / dee wreck see on / ess tah / en / mee /
boll see yo**.

12

Please don't tell anyone. I am with my wife's best friend.
No digas nada. Estoy con la mejor amiga de mi esposa.
No / dee gas / nar da. / Ess toy / con / la / meh whore / am eager / deh / mee / ess pose ah.

At the Chemist *Farmacia* Farmer see ah

I need a packet of plasters.
Necesito un paquete de tiritas.
Ness ess see toe / oon / pack et teh / deh / tea reet ass.

What remedy would you recommend for …?
Puede usted darme algo contra …?
Poo ed eh / ooze ted / dar meh / algo / contra …?

Migraine	*Migraña*	**Mee gran knee ya**
Indigestion	*Indigestión*	**Een dee hess tea on**
Lethargy	*Letargo*	**Let are go**
Rheumatism	*Reumatismo*	**Reh ooh mat tease mo**
Insomnia	*Insomnio*	**Een som knee oh**
Piles	*Hemorroides*	**Eh more oi dess**
Bad breath	*Mal aliento*	**Mal / ally en toe**

Menstruation pains.
Dolores de menstruación.
Dolores / deh / mens true assy on.

Mosquito bites.
Picaduras de mosquito.
Peek ah doo rass / de / moss key toe.

Crippling sunburn.
Quemadura de sol fuerte.
Keh ma doo rah / deh / sol / foo air teh.

Can you give me something for a pain in …? Then point.
Puede usted darme algo contra el dolor de …?
Poo ed eh / ooze ted / dar meh / algo / contra / ell / doll law / deh …?

I've got a headache.
Tengo dolor de cabeza.
Ten go / doll law / de / cab beth ah.

I have a fever.
Me siento febril.
Meh / see en toe / feb reel.

I've got a sore throat.
Tengo la garganta irritada.
Ten go / la / gar gan ta / ee ree tah da.

I've got a horrible cough.
Tengo una tos horrible.
Ten go / oon ah / toss / or ree bleh.

I'm very constipated.
Estoy muy estreñido.
Ess toy / moo ee / ess tren yee doe.

I've got intolerable diarrhoea.
Tengo una intolerable diarrea.
Ten go / oon ah / een toe leh rah bleh / dee ah reh ya.

I've got a boil on my backside.
Tengo un grano en el trasero.
Ten go / oon / gran oh / en ell / trass air oh.

I've got blisters.
Tengo los ampollas.
Ten go / loss / am po yass.

14

At the Doctor *Medico* **Meh Dick oh**

I have a serious – constant – spasmodic pain in the area of my:
Tengo un dolor grave – constante – espasmódico en mi:
Ten go / oon / doll law / gra veh – con stan teh – ess spaz moe dick oh – en / mee:

Ear	*Oído*	**Oh ee doe**
Eye	*Ojo*	**Oh ho**
Neck	*Cuello*	**Coo ay oh**
Shoulder	*Hombro*	**Om bro**
Chest	*Pecho*	**Petch oh**
Heart	*Corazón*	**Caw rah son**
Back	*Espalda*	**Ess pal dah**
Thigh	*Muslo*	**Moose low**
Knee	*Rodilla*	**Roe dee yah**
Ankle	*Tobillo*	**Toby yo**
Foot	*Pie*	Not like pork pie, but **pee eh**
Toe	*Dedo del pie*	**Day do / del / pee eh**
Rectum	*Recto*	**Wreck toe**
Genitals	*Genitales*	**Jenny tah lez**

I have had terrible stomach pains for the last week.
Tengo un dolor muy fuerte en el estómago desde una semana.
Ten go / oon / doll law / moo ee / foo air teh / en / ell / ess toe margo / des day / oon ah / sem anne ah.

I have been spitting blood.
Escupo sangre.
Ess coo po / san grey.

My poo-poo is black – brown – beige – green.
Mi caca está negra – marrón – beige – verde.
Mee / kacka / ess tah / neh grah – ma ron – beige – vair deh.

15

I have been accused of being a hypochondriac but I am sure
I am suffering from idiopathic thrombocytopenic purpura.
*Me acusan de ser hipocondríaco pero creo que tengo
púrpura trombocitopénica idiopática.*
**Meh / ak ooze anne / de / sair / ee poke on dree ark oh /
peh roe / kreh oh / keh / ten go / pour pour ah / trombo
sea toe pen knicker / idio pat ticker**.

I think I am going to die.
Me parece que me voy a morir.
Meh / pah ress eh / keh / meh / voy / ah / more ear.

At the Hospital   *Hospital* Oss pee tal

I need a bedpan urgently.
Necesito una cuña urgentemente.
**Ness essy toe / oon ah / coo knee ah / oor hen teh men
teh**.

I am in extreme pain. Could I have morphine?
Tengo un dolor muy intenso. Me podría dar morfina?
**Ten go / oon / doll law / moo ee / een ten so. / Meh / pod
ree ah / dar / more feena?**

That was nice. Could I have another shot?
Qué agradable! Me podría pinchar de nuevo?
**Keh / agra dab bleh! / Meh / pod ree ah / pinch are / deh /
noo eh vo?**

I think there are fleas inside my plaster.
Creo que hay pulgas dentro de mi escayola.
**Creh oh / keh / eye / pool gas / dent roe / deh / mee / ess
scar yola**.

16

Could I have another pillow?
Me podría dar otra almohada?
Meh / pod ree ah / dar / oat rah / almo ard ah?

I feel much better – worse – today.
Hoy me siento – mejor – peor.
Oy / meh / see en toe – meh whore – pay awe.

When can I leave?
Cuando me dan de alta?
Coo one doe / meh / dan / deh / al tah?

Could you give me another blanket bath tomorrow, nurse?
Enfermera, podría lavarme de nuevo mañana?
En fair meh rah, / pod ree ah / lav are meh / de / noo eh vo / man knee ah nah?

My mother-in-law is coming to visit me. Could you tell her I am in a coma.
Mi suegra viene a visitarme. Podría decirla que estoy en coma?
Mee / sue egg rah / vee any / ah / visit army. / Pod ree ah / deh sear la / keh / ess toy / en / coma?

17

At the Dentist *Dentista* Dent east ah

I have unbearable toothache.
Tengo un dolor de muelas terrible.
Ten go / oon / doll law / deh / moo ell arse / tear ee bleh.

A filling has fallen out.
Un empaste se ha caído.
Oon / empass stay / seh / ah / ka ee doe.

That hurts!
Me hace daño!
Meh / ass eh / dan knee oh!

Of course I want an anaesthetic.
Claro que quiero un anastésico.
Clah roe / keh / key air oh / oon / anne ass tess see co.

Where do I spit?
Dónde escupo?
Don deh / ess coop oh

Should my tooth have come out like that?
Es normal que se me haya caído el diente de esta manera?
Ess / normal / keh / say / meh / eye ah / ka ee doe / ell / dee en teh / deh / ess tah / man air ah?

At the Optician *Optica* Op ticker

I have broken my spectacles. Can you replace them?
He roto mis cristales. Podría ponerme unos nuevos?
Heh / roe toe / mees / chris tah les. / Pod ree ah / pon air meh / oon oss / noo eh vos?

18

I have lost one of my contact lenses.
He perdido una de mis lentillas.
Heh / pair dee doe / oon ah / de / mees / len tea yass.

It fell into the paella.
Se cayó en la paella.
Seh / kah yo / en / la / pie eh yah.

I am myopic – long sighted.
Tengo miopía – hipermetropía.
Ten go / mee oh pee ah – hee pair meh tro pee ah.

What chart where?
Qué pantalla, dónde?
Keh / pant ah yah, / don deh?

At the Police Station

La Comisaría **La / Com miss are ear**

The local police – *policía* (**polly sea ah**) – have been ordered to be tourist friendly, which they are if you are a shapely blonde. If not, use the following phrase at all times:

No / comprendo.
No comprendo.
I don't understand.

However, if your car has been broken into or towed away, or you have been mugged, the following will help.

My car has been broken into. They have stolen my:
Mi han robado cosas del coche. Se han llevado mi:
Mee / anne / rob ah doe / koss ass / dell / cotch eh. / Say / anne / yeh va doe / mee:

Luggage	*Equipaje*	**Eh key pa heh**
Briefcase	*Maleta*	**Ma letter**
Tools	*Herramientas*	**Air army en tass**
Laptop	*Portátil*	**Porter teel**
Dog	*Perro*	**Peh roe**

Digital camera. *Cámara digital.* **Cam ah rah / dee hee tal**.

Sixteen-year-old daughter.
Hija de dieciseis años.
Ee hah / de / dee essy say ease / an knee oss.

I have been mugged and they have taken my:
Me han asaltado y se han llevado mi:
Me / an / ass salt ah doe / ee / seh / an / yeah va doe / mee:

Bag	*Bolsa*	**Boll sah**
Wallet	*Cartera*	**Car terror**
Passport	*Pasaporte*	**Pass ah port eh**
Plane ticket	*Billete de avion*	**Bee yeah teh / de / ah vee on**
Trousers	*Pantalones*	**Pant ah low nez**
Wedding ring	*Anillo de boda*	**Annie oh / deh / boe dah**.

Credit cards.
Tarjeta de crédito.
Tar hetta / de / cred ee toe.

One million in cash.
Un millón en metálico.
Oon / milly on / en / metal lick oh.

Everything I have in the whole wide world.
Todo lo que tengo en el mundo.
Toe doe / low / keh / ten go / en / ell / moon doe.

Should you be arrested by mistake or for inappropriate behaviour, ask for your nearest Consulate (closed at weekends) thus:

Take me to the Consulate.
Lléveme al Consulado.
Yeah veh meh / al / Con soo lah doe.

I wish to speak to the Ambassador who is a personal friend
of mine.
Quiero hablar con el embajador, un íntimo amigo mío.
**Key ero / ab lar / con / ell / em bar hard door, / oon /
een tee mo / ah mee go / mee oh**.

Getting About

On Foot *A pie* **Ap / yea**

Which is the way to …?
Qué dirección para …?
Keh / dee wreck see on / para …?

You will get a reply that sounds like:

Allah / ease key air da.
A la izquierda.
Go to the left.

Allah / deh wretch ah.
A la derecha.
Go to the right.

Dee wreck toe.
Directo.
Go straight ahead.

Voo ell veh / ah trass.
Vuelve atrás.
Back that-a-way.

Ess tah / leh hoss / deh / ah key.
Está lejos de aquí.
It's far from here.

If you do not understand because of rural accents, try:

Can you show me where that is on this map?
Me puede enseñar dónde está en el mapa?
Meh / poo ed eh / en sen knee are / don deh / ess tah / en / ell / map ah?

Can you draw it for me on this piece of paper?
Me lo puede dibujar en este papel?
Meh / low / poo ed eh / dee boo har / en / ess teh / pa pell?

Oh dear! Where can I get a taxi?
Dios mio! Dónde puedo coger un taxi?
Dee oss / mee oh! / Don deh / poo ed oh / co hair / oon / taxi?

By Taxi *En Taxi* En / Taxi

In Spain the word for street, avenue, square, etc. comes first in an address and the number last, e.g: Number 10 Downing Street would be Street Downing Number 10. So for Number 10, Juan Carlos Street, you ask the driver for:

Calle Juan Carlos número diez, por favor.
Ka yeh / who won / car loss / noo meh roe / dee eth, / paw / fav awe.

After which you can settle back and let him rant about the incompetent playing of his favourite football team.

By Bus *En Autobús* En / out oh boos

All towns and cities in Spain are spelled and pronounced the same as in English except for the city of Seville, *Sevilla* (**Sev vee yah**) for reasons only known to those who live there.

I would like to go on a bus trip to Granada. How much is it?
Me gustaría ir a Granada en autobús. Cuánto vale?
Meh / goose ta ria / ear / ah / Granada / en / out oh boos. / Coo one toe / valley?

When does the bus leave?
A que hora sale el autobús?
Ah / keh / aura / sal eh / ell / out oh boos?

At what time does it get back?
A que hora regresa?
Ah / keh / aura / regress ah?

Can't it get back before?
No puede volver antes?
No / poo ed eh / vol vair / ant ez?

Is this the right bus for Salamanca?
Es éste el autobús que va a Salamanca?
Es / ess teh / ell / out oh boos / keh / vah / ah / Salamanca?

Which is the right bus for Salamanca?
Cuál es el autobús que va a Salamanca?
Coo al / ess / ell / out oh boos / keh / vah / ah / Salamanca?

Does this stop at the bullring?
Para cerca de la plaza de toros?
Para / sair ka / deh / la / plaza / de / tor ross?

23

Could you tell me where I get off?
Me podría decir dónde me bajo?
Meh / pod ree ah / deh sear / don deh / meh / ba hoe?

I was told this bus went to Salamanca.
Me dijeron que este autobús iba a Salamanca.
Meh / dee heron / keh / ess teh / out oh boos / ee bah / ah / Salamanca.

I am on the wrong bus. Please stop, I want to get off.
Me he subido en el autobús equivocado. Parar por favor, quiero bajarme.
Meh / heh / sue bee doe / en / ell / out oh boos / eh key vo car doe. / Par are / paw / fav awe, / key ero / bar har meh.

When is the next bus back to Madrid?
Cuándo es el próximo autobús de vuelta a Madrid?
Coo one doe / ess / ell / proxy mo / out oh boos / de / voo ell ta / ah / Madrid?

How long does it take?
Cuánto se tarda?
Coo one toe / seh / tar dah?

Is there any other way I can get to Madrid or Granada?
Hay otra manera de llegar a Madrid o Granada?
Eye / oat rah / man air ra / de / yeah gar / ah / Madrid / oh / Granada?

By Train *En Tren* En / Tran

| Station | *Estación* | **Ess tah see on** |
| Platform | *Andén* | **Anne den** |

24

Regionales **Reh hee oh nah lez** Stops at every station
Estrella **Ess tray yah** Night sleeper to anywhere
Diurno **Dee or no** Day sleeper for siestas

What time are the trains to Malaga?
A qué hora salen los trenes a Málaga?
Ah / keh / aura / sah len / loss / tren ehs / ah / Malaga?

One return ticket to Oviedo.
Un billete de vuelta a Oviedo.
Oon / bee yeah teh / de / voo ell ta / ah / Oh vee eh doe.

Two single tickets to Huelva.
Dos billetes de ida a Huelva.
Doss / bee yeah tehs / de / ee da / ah / Oo ell vah.

Which platform for Badajoz?
Qué andén es el de Badajoz?
Keh / Anne den / ess / ell / de / Bud ah hoz?

Does this train stop at many stations?
Para mucho este tren?
Para / moo cho / ess teh / tren?

Do I have to change?
Tengo que cambiar?
Ten go / keh / cam bee are?

I thought you said the train left at six.
Creí entender que este tren salía a las seis.
Cray ee / en ten dare / keh / ess teh / tren / sah lee ah / ah / lass / say ease.

It is now seven thirty.
Son las siete y media.
Son / lass / see eh teh / ee / med dee ah.

I wanted to get out at Valencia.
Quería bajarme en Valencia.
Keh ria / ba harm meh / en / Valencia.

Where does this train go to then?
A dónde va este tren?
Ah / don deh / va / ess teh / tren?

I know it's the wrong ticket!
Sé que tengo el billete equivocado!
Seh / keh / ten go / ell / bee yeah teh / eh key voe car doe!

How much more?
Cuánto más?
Coo one toe / mass?

Do you accept Morrocan currency?
Acepta monedas marroquíes?
Axe sep ta / mo ned ass / marrow key ez?

By Car *En Coche* En / Cotch eh

I want to hire a car.
Quiero alquilar un coche.
Key ero / al keel are / oon / cotch eh.

Do you have any other colours? My wife is superstitious about mauve.
Tienen otros colores? Mi mujer es supersticiosa con el malba.
Tea en en / oat ross / coll awe res? / Mee / moo hair / ess / sue pair stee see ossa / con / ell / malba.

Can I have a roof rack?
Tiene baca?
Tea any / backer?

26

Is there air conditioning?
Tiene aire acondicionado?
Tea any / ay reh / ah con dee see oh nah do?

What type of petrol does the car consume?
Qué tipo de gasolina consume este coche?
**Keh / tea po / de / gas oh lean ah / con sue meh / ess teh /
cotch eh?**

Sin plomo	**Sin plo mo**	Unleaded
Súper	**Super**	Super
Diesel	**Dee ezel**	Diesel

Could you fill her up, please.
Lleno, por favor.
Yeah no, / paw / fav awe.

Give me what you can for this amount of change.
Dame lo que puedas por este dinero.
**Dar meh / low / keh / poo ed ass / paw / ess teh / dean
air oh.**

Car Trouble

Problemas con el coche **Proe blem ass / con / ell / cotch eh**

The keys are locked inside the car.
El coche quedó cerrado con las llaves dentro.
**Ell / cotch eh / keh doe / seh rah doe / con / lass / yah
vez / dent roe.**

I have run out of petrol.
Me he quedado sin gasolina.
Meh / heh / keh dar doe / sin / gas oh lean ah.

It will not start.
No arranca.
No / ah ran car.

Where is the nearest garage for repairs?
Dónde está el garage con taller más próximo?
Don deh / ess tah / ell / ga ra heh / con / tah ee air / mas / proxy mo?

I have a puncture.
Tengo un pinchazo.
Ten go / oon / pinch ass so.

The engine is overheating.
El motor está recalentado.
Ell / motor / ess tah / wrecker len tah doe.

How long will it take?
Cuánto tardara?
Coo one toe / tar dar rah?

How long!
Cuánto!
Coo one toe!

28

Can't you do it any sooner than that?
Lo puedes hacer antes?
Low / poo ed des / ass air / anne tez?

How much do I owe you?
Cuánto te debo?
Coo one toe / teh / deb oh?

Are you sure? My car is not a Jaguar.
Está seguro de que es éste? Mi coche no es un Jaguar.
Ess tah / seh goo roe / de / keh / ess / ess teh? / Mee / cotch eh / no / ess / oon / Jaguar.

Where can I hire a motor scooter?
Dónde puedo alquilar una escúter?
Don deh / poo ed oh / al keel are / oon ah / ess scooter?

Parking

Aparcamiento **Ah park ah mee en toe**

I do not understand the ticket machine instructions.
No entiendo las instrucciones de la máquina de tickets.
No / en tee en doe / lass / een strook sea oh nez / de / la / mac keen nah / de / tee kets.

Which slot? Where?
Qué ranura? Dónde?
Keh / rah noo rah? / Don deh?

The machine does not work.
La máquina no funciona.
La / mac keen na / no / foonk sea oh nah.

The barrier will not go up.
La barrera no se levanta.
La / bar rare ah / no / seh / leh van tah.

I cannot find my car.
No encuentro mi coche.
No / en coo entro / mee / cotch eh.

I don't remember the number.
No recuerdo la matrícula.
No / wreck oo air doe / la / mat tree cool ah.

I will know it when I see it.
Lo reconoceré cuando lo vea.
Low / wreck oh no sair eh / coo one doe / low / veh ah.

I think a Barbie and Ken are on the back seat.
Creo que hay una Barbie y un Ken en el asiento trasero.
Kreh oh / keh / eye / oon ah / Barbie / ee / oon / Ken / en / ell / ass see en toe / tras air oh.

Road Rage

Furia al volante **Foo ree ah / al / vol an teh**
(Roman: fury at the steering wheel.)

Why don't you learn to drive?
Porque no aprendes a conducir, mamón?
Pork eh / no / ah pren des / ah con doo see er, / ma mon?

What the hell are you hooting at?
Equivalent: *Deja de tocar el pito hombre?*
Deh ha / deh / toe car / ell pee toe / om breh?
(Roman: Stop playing with the horn – *pito* means horn and willy).

30

How could I see the sign? There's a stupid van in the way.
Cómo voy a ver la señal? Hay una puta furgoneta en medio.
Como / voy / ah / vair / la / sen knee yal? / Eye / oon ah / poota / phoor go net ah / en / meh dee oh.

Get a move on!
Equivalent: *Parece que está pisando huevos!*
Par ess eh / keh / ess tah / pee sand oh / oo eh vos!
(Roman: Looks like you're treading on eggs – *huevos* means eggs and balls.)

I didn't know it was a one way street!
No sabía que era una calle de dirección única!
No / sab bee ah / keh / air ah / oon ah / car yea / deh / dee wreck sea on / oo knicker!

Choice words that could be shouted at you by Spanish drivers:

Cab ron!	*Cabrón!*	Bastard! (Roman: cuckold.)
Mee air da!	*Mierda!*	Shit!
Marry con!	*Maricón!*	Poofter!
Hilly / po / yass!	*Gilipollas!*	Dick head!

Ee ho / deh / poo tah!
Hijo de puta!
Son of a whore! (This is a very standard expletive.)

Meh / cargo / en / toe doe / low / keh / seh / moo eh veh!
Me cago en todo lo que se mueve!
I relieve myself on all that moves!

To all of which you can reply:

And the same to you!
Lo mismo digo!
Lo / mees mo / dee go!

By Boat *En Barco* **En / Bark oh**

I feel sick.
Me mareo.
Meh / marry oh.

Should the porthole be below sea level?
Es normal que la portilla este bajo el nivel del mar?
Ess / normal / keh / la / port tea yah / ess teh / bar ho / ell / knee vell / dell / mar?

I can't swim.
No sé nadar.
No / say / nad are.

Should we be at this angle?
Es normal que estemos tan inclinados?
Es / normal / keh / ess stem moss / tan / een clean are doss?

Have you got a life jacket?
Tiene un salvavidas?
Tea any / oon / salva vee dass?

Man overboard!
Hombre al agua!
Om breh / al / ah goo ah!

Getting a Bed

Five Star
There should be no need to speak Spanish in a five star hotel. Receptionists, head waiters, waiters, barmen bell-boys and chambermaids usually speak English.

Four Star
There should be no need to speak Spanish in a four star hotel. Recepionists, head waiters, and barmen usually speak English.

Three Star
There should be no need to speak Spanish in a three star hotel. The receptionists should speak English, the head waiter probably speaks English, and other members of the staff will understand you enough to help you out of any difficulties.

Two Star
The receptionist may be under the impression that he or she speaks English, but in fact is quite unintelligible. Best to arm yourself with the phrase book to get what you really want.

One Star
These hotels cater mainly for the natives. The owner-manager will deliberately not understand you, so it is best to prepare the following phrases:

Do you have a single room?
Tiene una habitación individual?
Tea any / oon ah / abby tassy on / een dee vee doo al?

I would like a double room for three nights.
Me gustaría una habitación doble para tres noches.
Me / goose ta ria / oon ah / abby tassy on / doe bleh / para / trez / no chess.

At what time do you stop serving breakfast?
Cuándo terminan de servir el desayuno?
Coo one doe / term mee nan / de / serve ear / ell / des ah you know?

Is there a lavatory on the same floor, or is it in the garden?
El cuarto de baño está en la misma planta, o en el jardín?
Ell / coo are toe / deh / ban nee yo / ess tah / en / la / mees ma / planta, / oh / en / ell / hard een?

There is no light bulb in my bedroom.
No hay bombilla en mi dormitorio.
No / eye / bom bee yah / en / mee / dormy tory oh.

There is no toilet paper.
No hay papel higiénico.
No / eye / pah pel / ee hee en knee co.

I am leaving now.
Me voy ahora mismo.
Meh / voy / ah aura / mees mo.

What are these charges for?
De qué son estos gastos?
Deh / keh / son / ess toss / gas toss?

But there is no phone in my room, and I have a mobile anyway.
Pero no hay teléfono en mi habitación, y yo tengo móvil.
Peh roe / no / eye / tel eff oh no / en / mee / abby tassy on, / ee / yo / ten go / mauve eel.

No Star
This will be a guest house. The owner manager genuinely will not understand a word you say, but try:

Is the water traditionally brown in this area?
Es normal que el agua salga marrón por aquí?
Ess / normal / keh / en / ell / ah goo ah / sal gah / ma ron / paw / ah key?

34

Does your son only dedicate himself to the electric guitar at night?

Tu hijo se dedica sólo a tocar la guitarra eléctrica por la noche?

Too / ee ho / seh / dead dicker / solo / ah / toe car / la / guitar rah / electric ah / paw / la / notch eh?

Are the holes in the mosquito net to let them in or out?

Los agujeros en la mosquitera son para que entren o salgan?

Los / ah goo heh ross / en / la / moss key terra / son / para / keh / en tren / oh / sal gan?

Getting Something to Eat and Drink

Fast Food *Comida Rapida* **Com mee da / Rap pee da**

Hamburger	*Hamburguesa*	**Am boor guesser**
Hot dog	*Perro caliente*	**Peh roe / cally en teh**
Ice Cream	*Helados*	**Eh lad doss**
Milk Shake	*Batido*	**Bah tee doe**
Small	*Pequeño*	**Peck en knee oh**
Medium	*Mediano*	**Med dee ah no**
Large	*Grande*	**Grand deh**

I would like: *Me gustaría:* **Meh / goose ta ria**:

A black coffee, please.

Un café solo, por favor.

Oon / caff eh / solo / paw / fav awe.

Coffee – with milk *Café con leche* **Caff eh / con / letch eh**
– with a dash of milk *con cortado* **con / cor tar doe**
– with a lot of milk *con sombra* **con / som bra**

Tea with milk.
Un té con leche.
Oon / teh / con / letch eh.

A cup of hot chocolate.
Una taza de chocolate caliente.
Oon ah / taza / deh / choco lah teh / cal lee en teh.

More sugar. *Más azúcar.* **Mass ah zoo car**.

A sandwich *Un bocadillo de:* **Oon / bock ah dee yo / deh**:

ham *jamón* **hammon**; cheese *queso* **keh so**; salami *salchichón* **sal chee chon**; prawn *gambas* **gum bass**; tuna *atún* **ah toon**

I would like to try the tapas.
Quiero probar las tapas.
Key ero / prob are / lass / tapas.

Is that a potato omelette?
Esta es una tortilla española?
Ess tah / ess / oon ah / tor tea yah / ess pan yola?

Are the things in brown sauce meat balls?
Eso en la salsa marrón son albóndigas?
Esso / en / la / salsa / ma ron / son / al bond ee gas?

I think I'd prefer the red peppers.
Prefiero tomarme los pimientos rojos.
Preh fee eh roe / tom army / loss / pee mee en toss / roh hoss.

Wow! An iced beer, quick!
Madre mía! / Una cerveza fresca, rápido!
Mad reh / mee ah! / Oon ah / sair vez ah / fres scar, / rap pee doe!

Essential Questions to Waiters

| Waiter! | *Camarero!* | **Cam ah rare oh!** |
| Waitress! | *Camarera!* | **Cam ah rare ah!** |

Do you have a garlic-free zone?
Tiene una zona sin ajo?
Tea any / oon ah / zon ah / sin / ah ho?

Could you recommend a good local wine?
Puede usted recomendarme un buen vino del país?
Poo ed eh / ooze ted / wreck oh mend army / oon / boo en / vee no / dell / pah ees?

A glass of red wine at room temperature.
Un tinto del tiempo.
Oon / tin toe / dell / tea em poe.

A glass of white wine.
Un blanco.
Oon / blank oh.

37

A glass of sherry.
Un vaso de Jerez.
Oon / va zo / deh / Heh ress.

A stiff brandy.
Un cognac fuerte.
Oon / cognac / foo air teh.

And another one, please.
Y otro más, por favor.
Ee / oat roe / mass, / paw / fav awe.

I think I'll try the almond liqueur.
Voy a probar el licor de almendras.
Voy / ah / prob are / ell / lee caw / deh / al men drass.

Apricot liqueur? Why not?
Licor de albaricoque? Por qué no?
Lee caw / de / al barry cocky? / Por / keh / no?

A large glass of mineral water, please.
Un gran vaso de agua mineral, por favor.
Oon / gran / var zo / deh / ah goo ah / mean air al, / paw / fav awe.

| Sparkling | *Con gas* | **Con gas** |
| Still | *Sin gas* | **Sin gas** |

I'd like the bill please.
La cuenta, por favor.
La / coo went ah, / paw / fav awe.

Is the tip included?
Está incluida la propina?
Ess tah / een clue ee dah / la / prop pee nah?

38

Are you sure this is correct?
Seguro que esto es correcto?
Seh goo roe / keh / ess toe / ess / co wreck toe?

Slow Food *Comida Lenta* **Com mee da / Lent ta**

Lunch   *Almuerzo*   **Al moo air zo**
Dinner   *Cena*   **Senna**

A mixed salad, to start.
Una ensalada mixta para empezar.
Oo nah / en salad ah / mix tah / para / em pez are.

Followed by the stuffed peppers, then the chicken.
Seguido por los pimientos rellenos, y después el pollo.
**Seg ee doe / paw / loss / pee me en toss / ray en oss, / ee /
dess poo ess / ell / po yo.**

I have been waiting a long time for my food.
Hace mucho que espero la comida.
Ass eh / moo cho / keh / ess peh roe / la / co mee da.

What do you mean the chef's having a siesta?
Qué quieres decir que el cocinero se está tomando una siesta?
**Keh / key air ess / dess ear / keh / ell / co seen air oh /
seh / ess tah / toe man doe / oon ah / siesta?**

Then I'll have the cold salmon.
Entonces, yo quiero el salmón fresco.
En ton sess, / yo / key ero / ell / sall mon / fresco.

Have you got a doggy bag?
Tiene una bolsita para el perro?
Tea any / oon ah / bol see tah / para / ell / peh roe?

Getting Service

At the Newsagents *Periódicos* **Perry odd ee coss**
(The tobacconist, *Estanco* **Ess stan co**, also sells stamps.)

Do you have this guide book in English?
Tiene guías locales en inglés?
Tea any / goo we ass / low car les / en / in glez?

Have you any maps of the city – town – district?
Tiene mapas de la ciudad – del pueblo – del distrito?
**Tea any / map ass / deh / la / see oo dad – dell / poo ebb
low – dell / dee street oh?**

I'll have these postcards and the stamps for them to get to:
Me llevaré estas postales y unos cuantos sellos para:
**Meh / yeh vah ray / ess tass / po star les / ee / ooh noss /
coo anne toss / say oss / para:**

Great Britain *Gran Bretaña* **Gran / Bret anne knee yah**
United States *Los Estados Unidos* **Loss / Ess star doss /
Oo knee doss**
Australia *Australia* **Ow strah lee ah**
Ireland *Irlanda* **Ear land ah**

Do you have any nudie magazines?
Tiene revistas eróticas?
Tea any / rev east ass / eh roe teak ass?

I wasn't trying to steal it, I just didn't want my wife to
know I was buying it.
*No intentaba robarlo, es que no quería que mi mujer se
diese cuenta que yo quería comprarlo.*
**No / een ten tar bar / rob are low, / ess / keh / no / keh
ria / keh / mee / moo hair / seh / dee ess eh / coo went ah /
keh / yo / keh ria / com prah low.**

At the Post Office *Correos* Cor eh oss

Pillar boxes are yellow with slots for:
LOCAL = Local; CIUDAD = City; EXTRANJERO = Abroad

How much is a stamp for this to: …?
Cuánto vale un sello para: …?
Coo one toe / valley / oon / say oh / para: …?

Which window do I go to then?
A qué ventanilla debo ir?
Ah / keh / vent ah knee ah / debo / ear?

I have just been there and they told me to come here!
Acabo de estar allí y me dijeron que viniese aquí!
Ack ah boe / de / ess star / ay ee / ee / meh / dee heron / keh / vee knee ess eh / ah key!

I wish to register this parcel.
Quiero certificar este paquete.
Key ero / sir tee fee car / ess teh / pack ket teh.

This packet is fragile. Please be careful.
Este paquete es frágil. Tenga cuidado por favor.
Ess teh / packet eh / ess / fra heel. / Ten gah / coo ee dah doe / paw / fav awe.

It wasn't leaking before I handed it to you.
No goteaba antes de habérselo entregado.
No / got ay ah bah / anne tez / deh / ab air sell oh / en treg are doe.

Could I have it back, please?
Me lo podriá devolver, por favor?
Meh / low / pod ree ah / devolve air, / paw / fav awe?

41

At the Bank *Banco* Banko

The cash point has swallowed my card.
El cajero automático se ha comido mi tarjeta.
Ell / ka hair roe / ow toe mat ee co / say / ah / com mee doe / mee / tah het tah.

It worked yesterday.
Ayer funcionaba.
Eye ee air / foon sea own abba.

No, I do not think I have spent my limit.
No, no creo haber gastado mi limite.
No, / no / kreh oh / ab air / gas tar doe / mee / lee meat teh.

Then can you change these travellers cheques?
Entonces puede cambiar estos cheques de viajes?
En ton sess / poo ed eh / cam bee are / ess toss / check kez / de / vee ah hez?

What is the rate of exchange?
A cuánto está el cambio?
Ah / coo one toe / ess tah / ell / cam bee oh?

Can I see the manager?
Puedo ver al gerente?
Poo ed doe / vair / al / heh rent eh?

Could I ring my bank at home?
Podría llamar a mi banco en mi país?
Pod ree ah / ya mar / ah / mee / bank oh / en / mee / pa ease?

Where do I sign?
Dónde firmo?
Don deh / fear mo?

At the Barber's in Seville

El Barbero de Sevilla **Ell / Bar bay roe / de / Se vee yah**

Could you just trim it a little?
Puede cortarme un poco?
Poo ed eh / court army / oon / poke oh?

Not too short, and a little bit off the sides.
No muy corto y un poco por los lados.
No / moo ee / court toe / ee / oon / poke oh / paw / loss / lad doss.

Were you trained as a hairdresser in the army?
Fuiste entrenado como peluquero en la mili?
Foo east teh / en tren ah doe / kom oh / pell loo keh roe / en / la / mee lee?

At the Hairstylist

La Peluquería **La / Peh loo keh rear**

Shampoo and blow dry please.
Champú y secado por favor.
Shampoo / ee / seck ah doe / paw / fav awe.

I'd like to change the colour of my hair.
Me gustaría cambiar el color de mi pelo.
Meh / goose ta ria / cam bee are / ell / col law / de / mee / pell oh.

Blonde – Brunette – Auburn – Green and Silver
Rubia – Morena – Pelirroja – Verde y Platino
Roo bee yah – Mo wren oh – Pelly roh ha – Ver deh / ee – Plat tea no

But I didn't want it cut at all!
Pero no quería que me lo cortase!
Pear oh / no / keh ria / keh / meh / low / caw tar seh!

Do you sell wigs?
Vende pelucas?
Venn day / peh look ass?

Having Fun

Sightseeing   *Las Vistas*   Las / Veast ass

At what time does the gallery – museum – open?
A qué hora abre esta galería – museo?
Ah / keh / aura / ab reh / ess tah / gal er ee yah – moos eh oh?

Is there a tour for this building?
Hay un tour para este edificio?
Eye / oon / tour / para / ess teh / eddy fee see oh?

When does it start?
Cuándo comienza?
Coo one doe / co me enza?

But that was an hour ago!
Pero eso fue hace una hora!
Pair oh / esso / foo eh / ass eh / oon ah / aura!

Are you saying they've closed the cathedral for yet another
procession?
*Me está diciendo que han cerrado la catedral para otra
procesión?*
**Meh / ess tah / dee see end oh / keh / anne / sair ah doe /
la / cat eh dral / para / oat rah / pro say see on?**

Can I climb to the top of this tower?
Puedo subir a la cima de la torre?
Poo ed oh / sue beer / ah / la / sea ma / de / la / torr eh?

Can anyone hear me down there? The door has jammed!
Me pueden escuchar abajo? La puerta está atascada!
**Meh / poo ed den / ess coo char / ab ah ho? / La / poo
air ta / ess tah / atter scar da!**

I suffer from vertigo!
Suffro de vertigo!
Sue fro / de / vair tee go!

What if I miss the mattress?
Que pasa si no llego al colchon?
Keh / pasa / see / no / yego / al / col chon?

At the Bullfight

Corrida de toros **Caw reader / deh / tor ross**

I would like a seat on the shady side of the ring.
Quiero una entrada a la sombra.
Key ero / oon ah / en trah dah / ah / la / som bra.

(The sunny side – *sol* – is cheaper, but will be hot.)

The following should be shouted with gusto every time the
toreadors dodge the bull's sharp horns:

Olé! **Oh leh!** Go for it!

Along with the other spectators you should flap a white
handkerchief about in the air moderately, energetically, or
frantically, depending on your opinion of the matador's

performance. When the bull is killed the matador might be awarded:

Una oreja **Oon ah / awe reh ha** One ear – if he's done well.

Dos orejas **Doss / awe reh hass** Two ears – if he's done really well.

Dos orejas y el rabo **Doss / awe reh hass / ee / ell / rab oh** Two ears and the tail – if he's done brilliantly.

And when he is carried out of the ring, shoulder-high, and showered with flowers and sundry garments, you should join in and shout: *Viva!*

At Pamplona *En Pamplona* **En / Pam ploe nah**

Down which street do they let the bulls run free?
Por cuál calle dejan salir a los toros?
Paw / coo al / cah yeah / deh han / sal ear / ah / loss / tor ross?

This one? When?
Esta? Cuándo?
Ess tah? / Coo one doe?

Good Grief! That's now!
Jolín! Ahora!
Ho lean! / Ah aura!

Yes, I would like to sit down, but I will need a pile of very soft cushions.
Me gustaría sentarme, pero en una pila de cojines suaves.
Meh / goose ta ria / sent army / pair oh / en / oon ah / peel ah / de / co he nez / sue ah vez.

At the Fiesta *La Fiesta* La / Fiesta

Your donkey is standing on my foot.
Tu burro me está pisando el pie.
Too / boo roe / meh / ess tah / pee sand oh / ell / pee eh.

What spectacular fireworks!
Que fuegos artificiales tan espectaculares!
**Keh / foo egg oss / art tee fee see ah lez / tan / es speck
tack coo la rez!**

Don't worry, my hair is only a bit singed.
No se preocupe, mi pelo sólo está un poco quemado.
**No / seh / pray ock coop eh, / mee / pello / solo / ess tah /
oon / poke oh / keh ma doe.**

At the Swimming Pool *La Piscina* La / Pee seen ah

Which is the deep end?
Cuál es la punta más profunda?
Coo al / ess / la / poon tah / mass / pro foon dah?

You were wrong.
Te equivocaste.
Teh / eh key vo cast eh.

No really, it's only a bump.
No de verdad, solo es un chichón.
No / deh / vair dad, / solo / ess / oon / chee chon.

Have you any aspirin?
Tienes aspirina?
Tea en ess / as pee reen ah?

On the Beach *La Playa* La / Plah yah

I would like a beach umbrella.
Me gustaría una sombrilla.
Meh / goose ta ria / oon ah / som bree yah.

And under it a beach bed.
Y debajo, una tumbona.
Ee / deh bah ho, / oon ah / toom bone ah.

That's my lilo!
Esta es mi colchoneta!
Ess tah / ess / mee / colch oh net ah!

Could your children play somewhere else?
Podrían vuestros niños jugar en otra parte?
Pod ree an / voo est ross / knee knee yoss / who gar / en / oat rah / party?

Should I beware of jelly fish?
Tengo que tener precaución con las medusas?
Ten go / keh / ten air / pray cow see on / con / lass / meh doo sass?

...som bree yah

48

How much is a pedalo?
Cuánto vale un pédalo?
Coo one toe / valley / oon / pay dah low?

Yes, of course I've water skied before.
Claro que he esquiado sobre el agua antes.
Clah roe / keh / eh / ess key ah doe / sob reh / ell / ah goo ah / anne tez.

Can you get the stretcher closer to the water?
Puede acercar la camilla más al agua?
Poo eddy / ah sir car / la / cami ya / mass / al / ah goo ah?

Shopping   *De Compras*   De / Com prass

Where is the street market?
Dónde está el mercadillo?
Don deh / ess tah / ell / mare car dee yo?

Does the flamenco doll come with a partner?
La muñeca de flamenco viene con pareja?
La / moon knee ecka / deh / flamenco / vee any / con / par reh ha?

How much is this?
Cuánto es éste?
Coo one toe / ess / ess teh?

Is that your best price?
Es tu mejor precio?
Ess / too / meh whore / press see yo?

I'll take it.
Me lo llevaré.
Meh / low / ye va reh.

I'll leave it.
Lo dejaré.
Low / deh ha reh.

I came by before and I want the Toledo bracelet after all.
Estuve aquí antes y quiero el brazalete de Toledo.
Ess too veh / ah key / anne tez / ee / key ero / ell / bra za letter / deh / Toledo.

No, I can't afford another one.
No, no tengo bastante dinero para otro.
No, / no / ten go / bass stan tay / dean air oh / para / oat roe.

I don't have any more money.
No tengo más dinero.
No / ten go / mass / dean air oh.

Do you have another castanet keyring?
Tiene otro llavero castañuela?
Tea any / oat roe / ya vair oh / cass stan noo ella?

Which souvenir is typical of this area?
Qué souvenir es típico de esta zona?
Keh / souvenir / ess / tea pee co / deh / ess tah / zonnah?

I don't think the straw donkey will fit in my suitcase.
No creo que el burro de paja quepa en mi maleta.
No / creh oh / keh / ell / boo roe / deh / pa hah / kay pa / en / mee / mal letter.

At the Boutique *La Boutique* La / Boutique eh

May I try this on?
Puedo probármelo?
Poo ed doe / pro bar mellow?

Where is the changing room?
Dónde está el probador?
Don deh / ess tah / ell / pro bar door?

I don't like the colour.
No me gusta el color.
No / meh / goose ta / ell / col law.

It doesn't fit me.
No me cabe.
No / meh / cab eh.

Do you have a bigger size?
Tiene uno más grande?
Tea any / ooh no / mass / gran deh?

It is too big – too small – too tight.
Es demasiado grande – pequeño – pegado.
**Ess / deh mass see ah doe / grand eh – peck ken knee
yo – peg ah doe.**

Listen to me please! I can't get the zip undone.
Oigame, por favor! No puedo desabrochar la cremallera.
**Oig ah meh! / paw / fav awe! / No / poo ed doe / dess ah
brotch ah / la / crem ah year ah.**

Don't worry. I'll pay for the damage.
No se preocupe. Le pagaré los daños.
**No / seh / pray oh coo pay. / Leh / pag are eh / loss / dan
knee oss.**

At the Disco   *El Disco*   El / Dees co

My name is .... What's yours?
Me nombre es ...... Y el tuyo?
Mee / nom bray / ess ...... Ee / ell / too yo?

What did you say?
Que a dicho?
Keh / ah / dee cho?

Sorry. Can't hear a thing!
Lo siento. No te oigo!
Low / see en toe. / No / teh / oy go!

At the Club   *El Club*   El / Kloob

For boys: *chicos*   cheek oss

Do you come here often?
Vienes aquí a menudo?
Vee en ness / ah key / ah / men oo doe?

Are you alone?
Estás sola?
Ess tass / so lah?

Does your brother always accompany you?
Está tu hermano siempre contigo?
Ess tah / too / air man oh / see em preh / con tea go?

Is there any way we can get rid of him?
Hay alguna manera de librarse de él?
Eye / al goon ah / man air ah / de / lee bra seh / deh / ell?

Give us a kiss.
Dame un beso.
Dah meh / oon / bess oh.

For girls: *chicas* **cheek ass**

I am not alone. I'm with my boyfriend.
No estoy sola. Estoy con mi novio.
No / ess toy / sola. / Ess toy / con / mee / no vee oh.

The big one with the bald head and tattoos.
El calvo grande con tatuajes.
Ell / calvo / grand eh / con / tat too are hez.

He eats little boys like you, so buzz off.
El come pequeños niños como tu, asi que largate.
Ell / co may / peck ken yos / knee knee oss / como / too, / ass see / keh / larger teh.

At the Massage Parlour

La Massaje **La / Mass ah heh**

I'd like a massage.
Quiero un masaje.
Key ero / oon / mass ah heh.

How much is the session?
Cuánto por una sesión?
Coo one toe / paw / oon ah / sessy on?

Can you do that again?
Puede hacerlo otra vez?
Poo ed eh / ass air low / oat rah / vez?

53

Sex *Haciendo el Amor* Ass see endo / ell / Ah more

Mature Female to Toy Boy:

I love that devil-may-care look in your eyes.
Me encanta esa mirada de niño extraviado e inocente en tus ojos.
Meh / en canter / ess ah / mee rada / deh / knee knee yo / ex travvy ah doe / eh / een oh sent eh / en / toos / oh hoss.

Do you work out or is that your natural build?
Haces ejercicio o eres naturalmente así?
Ass ess / eh hair sea sea oh / oh / air ress / nah too ral men teh / ass see?

Have you finished? So soon?
Has terminado? Tan pronto?
Ass / term mee nah doe? Tan / pronto?

Sugar Daddy to Nymphette:

Hello, my dear. Can I buy you an ice cream – glass of wine – bottle of vodka?
Hola jovencita, te puedo comprar un helado – copa de vino – botella de vodka?
Ola / ho ven sea tah, / teh / poo ed doe / com prar / oon / ell lad oh – copper / deh / vee no – bot ay yah / deh / vodka?

Are you on the pill?
Tomas la píldora?
Tom ass / la / pill dora?

Won't be a minute. I'll just get my viagra.
No tardaré nada cariño. Ahora vuelvo con el viagra.
No / tar dar eh / nah dah / careen knee yo. / Ah aura / voo ell vo / con / ell / viagra.

Young Stud to Bimbo:

Are you from around here?
Eres de aquí?
Air ez / deh / ah key?

Like to show me the sights then?
Me enseñas las vistas entonces?
Meh / en sen knee ass / lass / veast ass / en ton sess?

All right darling? (Literally: How goes it aunty?)
Qué pasa tía?
Keh / pass ah / tee ah?

Sweet Young Thing to Macho Male:

Don't do that.
No hagar eso.
No / ag are / esso.

Leave me alone.
Déjame.
Deh ha meh.

I don't fancy you.
No me gustas.
No / meh / goose tass.

Please go away.
Por favor vete.
Paw / fav awe / veh teh.

I warn you. I have a dangerously contagious disease.
Te advierto. Tengo una enfermedad muy contagiosa.
Teh / add vee air toe. / Ten go / oon ah / en fair meh dad / moo ee / con tag ee oh sa.

Public Notices You May Come Up Against

CERRADO	Closed
SALDO	Sale
ASCENSOR	Lift/Elevator
ESPEREN	Wait
SALIDA	Exit
NO ESTACIONARSE	No Parking
NO BAÑARSE	No Bathing
NO ESCUPIR	No Spitting
SIN SALIDA	No Exit
PROHIBIDO EL PASO	No Entry
PROHIBIDO FUMAR	No Smoking
BOMBEROS	Fire Brigade
UNI-DIRECCIONAL	One Way Street
PASO DE PEATONES	Pedestrian Crossing
PASO A NIVEL	Level Crossing
NO ASOMARSE	Do Not Lean Out
NO TOCAR	Do Not Touch
AGUA POTABLE	Drinking Water
SERVICIOS / ASEOS	Toilets
SEÑORAS	Ladies
CABALLEROS	Gentlemen
LIBRE	Free/Vacant
OCUPADO	Occupied/Engaged

FUERA DE SERVICIO	Out of Order
EMPUJAR	Push
TIRAR	Pull
LEVANTAR	Lift/Raise
PULSAR	Press (the bell)
PRIVADO	Private
PELIGRO	Danger
VENENO	Poison
CUIDADO CON EL PERRO	Beware of the Dog

NB: in Spain hot water = CALIENTE is marked 'C' on a tap, and cold water = FRIA is marked 'F'

Phrases You May Hear

Keh / key air ez?
Qué quieres?
What do you want?

Voo ell vay / mass / tar deh.
Vuelve más tarde.
Come back later.

Pa gay / paw / addle anne tah doe.
Pague por adelantado.
You must pay in advance.

Ess toe / no / ess / bass stan teh.
Esto no es bastante.
That is not enough.

Toe das / noo ess tras / abby tassy oh nez – mess ass – ess tan / oh coo pa das.
Todas nuestras habitaciones – mesas – están ocupadas.
All our rooms – tables – are taken.

Ah / yeg ah doe / dem mass see ah doe / tar deh.
Ha llegado demasiado tarde.
You are too late.

No / nos / een coom beh.
No nos incumbe.
That is not our concern.

Keh / passer / ah key?
Qué pasa aquí?
What is happening here?

Sue / nom bray / paw / fav awe.
Su nombre por favor.
Your name, please.

Key en / ess / ell / seag yen teh?
Quién es el siguiente?
Who is next?

Addle anty.
Adelante.
Come in.

Ess pear eh / paw / fav awe.
Espere por favor.
Please wait.

No / seh.
No sé.
I don't know.

Keh / pee so?
Qué piso?
Which floor do you want?

Seh / ah / eh key voe car doe.
Se ha equivocado.
You have the wrong number.

En / ess teh / momento / no / le / poo ed oh / ah ten dare.
En este momento no le puedo attender.
At present there is no one to answer your call.

No / leh / poo ed oh / ah you dar.
No le puedo ayudar.
I cannot help you.

No / eem port ah.
No importa.
It doesn't matter.

Sair vee see oh / no / een clue wee doe.
Servicio no incluído.
Service is not included.

No / tea any / cam bee oh?
No tiene cambio?
Have you no change?

Vah leh.
Vale.
Okay.

No / meh / preh goon tess. **/ Yo / tum poke oh / soy / deh / ah key**.
No me preguntes. Yo tampoco soy de aquí.
Don't ask me. I'm a stranger here myself.

Last Words

See you.
Hasta la vista.
Ass ta / la / veast sta.

See you sometime.
Hasta luego.
Ass ta / loo egg oh.

Please say that again, but more slowly.
Puedes repetirlo, más lento.
Poo ed dess / rep pet tear low, / mass / lent oh.

Is there anyone here who speaks English?
Hay alguien que hable inglés?
Eye / alg yen / keh / ah bleh / in gless?